LAWN LOVE

"A soothing green, velvety lawn is a rolled out carpet inviting your friends to enter your home. It also provides the perfect backdrop for the costumed and performing shrubs, flowers, and trees which say welcome to your guests. No home can be complete without a lovely lawn. So let's start right and build a lawn that will be admired and easy to maintain."

—JERRY BAKER

MAKE FRIENDS WITH YOUR LAWN
was originally published by Simon and Schuster.

Books by Jerry Baker

I Never Met a House Plant I Didn't Like
Jerry Baker's Back to Nature Almanac
Jerry Baker's Second Back to Nature Almanac
Jerry Baker's Third Back to Nature Almanac
Jerry Baker's Bicentennial Gardener's Almanac
Make Friends with Your Lawn
Make Friends with Your Vegetable Garden
Plants Are Like People
Talk to Your Plants

Published by POCKET BOOKS

MAKE FRIENDS WITH YOUR

LAWN

JERRY BAKER

Designed and Edited by Charles Cook

PUBLISHED BY POCKET BOOKS NEW YORK

MAKE FRIENDS WITH YOUR LAWN

Simon and Schuster edition published 1973

POCKET BOOK edition published April, 1976

This POCKET BOOK edition includes every word contained in
the original, higher-priced edition. It is printed from brand-
new plates made from completely reset, clear, easy-to-read type.
POCKET BOOK editions are published by
POCKET BOOKS,
a division of Simon & Schuster, Inc.,
A GULF+WESTERN COMPANY
630 Fifth Avenue,
New York, N.Y. 10020.
Trademarks registered in the United States
and other countries.

Standard Book Number: 671-80303-4.
Library of Congress Catalog Card Number: 73-1201.
This POCKET BOOK edition is published by arrangement
with Simon & Schuster, Inc. Copyright, ©, 1973, by Jerry
Baker. All rights reserved. This book, or portions thereof,
may not be reproduced by any means without permission of
the original publisher: Simon & Schuster, Inc.,
630 Fifth Avenue, New York, New York 10020.
Printed in the U.S.A.

Contents

MAKE FRIENDS WITH YOUR LAWN

GRANT HEILMAN

Lawn Love

A soothing green, velvety lawn is a rolled out carpet inviting your friends to enter your home. It also provides the perfect backdrop for the costumed and performing shrubs, flowers and trees which say welcome to your guests. No home can be complete without a lovely lawn. So let's start right and build a lawn that will be admired and easy to maintain.

You Can't Spell Lawn Love Without Three P's

If you've talked to the grounds keeper at the country club, you know that a perfect lawn is a work of science and daily care. And if you're a busy guy like me, you can't use all those golden hours at home pulling dandelions and mothering a lot of delicate grass blades.

Now don't be discouraged. You can have that beautiful lawn if you simply remember the three "P's." Here they are:

PRIDE
PERSISTENCE
PATIENCE

If you'll paint these words on your toolshed door and teach them to the kiddies, your thumb will be the greenest on the block.

PRIDE. Take pride in all you do. If you can't do a job to the best of your ability, don't do it. There's no joy in gardening if you can't throw out your chest a little at the close of the day.

To have a great lawn you need the three P's—Pride, Persistence and Patience.

PERSISTENCE. The old saying that quitters never win is doubly true when working with Mother Nature. She's going to give you some hard times to see if you've got the stick-to-itiveness to succeed. Don't give up.

PATIENCE. You can't hurry the sun. Wishing won't make spring arrive a day earlier. So relax and work with Mother Nature's timetable.

Your lawn, believe it or not, is much like the hair on your head. What impressions does a person make with shaggy, unbrushed, unwashed hair? About the same impression you'll make if you let your grass grow like a field of timothy full of cockle burrs. Don't have a "hippie" lawn. Make your house smile with pride by giving your lawn regular good grooming care.

Think of your lawn as if it were the hair on your head.

Thatch

What is thatch? It's what you could call lawn dandruff. Every time you ride your shiny mower over the grass, the clippings you don't collect leave a thin layer of mulch. The clippings, along with other debris, build up into a matted, rotting layer we call thatch.

Lawn dandruff or thatch is a good place for Freddy Fungus to make a home. Fungus kills the roots and will make your lawn look like a bald head. As thatch builds up, gets thick and tightly matted, it keeps the rain and plant food from getting through. This robs Benny the Blade of his daily nourishment and refreshing drink of cool water.

Give Your Lawn a Dandruff Treatment

OK, so thatch is one of the bad guys, what can be done about him? The number one solution is prevention. Get a grass catcher on your mower and collect the clippings. These will make a beneficial mulch around your peonies.

To get rid of old ugly lawn dandruff that is already a problem, use one of these three techniques:

1. Purchase a lawn groom rake especially designed to do the job. It has many little half-moon-shaped blades with sharp edges that cut through the tangled thatch. For a small lawn this rake and a little old-fashioned work will do fine.

2. You can make your rotary lawn mower into a power dethatcher by simply attaching an inexpensive roto rake bar to the blade. It's a good way to go, but let me give you a tip. Start the mower on a bare

*A power rake or renovator can be rented from local
equipment rental shops.*

surface, preferably on concrete or on an asphalt
driveway, then keep the mower moving at an even
pace back and forth across your lawn. Don't stop and
admire the lilacs. The continuous action in one spot
will do serious damage to the grass roots.

3. You might prefer to use a power rake or renovator. This is a specialized piece of equipment which is
better to rent from your local tool rental shop than
to purchase. A renovator will give your lawn a great
dandruff treatment—but use it with care and con-
centration.

Dethatching your lawn has fringe benefits too. It
stimulates root growth, giving your grass a fresh,
healthier color and a good appetite.

You'll be surprised to discover that 1,000 square feet
of lawn will yield six or eight garbage cans full of old
dead grass.

Remember good ecology means using waste products. So don't leave the thatch for the garbage man to
haul off. Start a compost heap or spread it around the
posies or around the tomato plants to conserve moisture
and keep out the weeds.

Remember that your lawn won't respond to medicine
and food until you get rid of the thatch. Dethatch your
lawn in the cool-weather states in April, June and September. In the West and South, October is a good time.

Getting back to our comparison between your lawn
and the hair on your head, let's talk some more about
good grooming care. Most important to a clean and
healthy head of hair is a sparkling shampoo.

And that's exactly what I want you to do for your
lawn. Right! A good sudsy shampoo will make Benny
the Blade stand tall and sing away the blues. Professional greens superintendents, like the one at your golf
club, treat greens with a surfactant to relieve surface
tension.

As a child, did you ever spit into the dust and watch
it sit there in a ball and not soak in? This is due to
surface tension.

"Gotta Wash That Thatch Right Outta My Grass"

Shampooing your lawn with a mild solution of soap and water allows the gentle rain, or water from your sprinkler, to break though this invisible barrier. You may buy the most expensive and best fertilizer—and you should buy the best—only to be disappointed with the results. It just might be that dandruff and a dirty scalp are keeping the nitrogen from getting down deep where the roots are feeding. Your money may be floating down the sewer to fatten the weeds and algae in your favorite fishing hole.

To apply a shampoo to your lawn, use a hose-end type lawn sprayer. One ounce of liquid soap, mixed with ten gallons of water, is enough to cover 1,500 square feet of lawn.

Get ahead! Give your lawn a scalp treatment.

How and Why

I like to use a biodegradable liquid dish soap. A mild soap that does not contain oil or harsh detergents is best.

Shampoo your lawn in the North soon after the snow is gone; in the West when the rains stop. In the South anytime in the spring is a good time to begin a regular shampoo program. Throughout the growing season Benny will love you if you give him a clean bath at least once a month.

I told you how shampoo would relieve surface tension. There are other good reasons for shampooing.

Your grass has pores and cells that allow the plant to manufacture food through the process of photosynthesis. These pores can get clogged by soot and dust that cling to the surface, causing the plant to become anemic and turn yellow or pale. Shampooing keeps your grass pores open and free of dust and soot. Also, the stickiness of the soap holds moisture longer. This saves having to water so often.

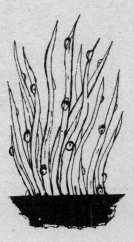

Bio-degradable soap only for this job please.

Benny the Blade says—
"When I'm shampooed I
fairly sparkle."

A regular lawn-washing program, such as I use on my lawn, stretches your fertilizer dollar. The soap acts as a spreader-sticker, catching the nitrogen in your fertilizer before it is washed out of its regular carrier. By "regular carrier" I mean the bulk material the fertilizer manufacturer uses to hold or carry the nitrogen.

Soap also makes your weed killer more effective by helping it stick to the grass where it can do the maximum good.

What will Bugsby the Bug think of your shampoo treatment? Well, bugs don't like the taste of soap any better than you do. This simple shampoo will act as a mild insecticide. When it becomes necessary to use an insecticide for a specific problem, this film of soap will hold the solution on the blades of grass where it's needed.

All I ask you to do is try it. You'll see how your lawn sparkles and beams like a baby after a bubble bath. Your lawn will be happy and healthy and your neighbors will soon quit laughing as you get out the bubble machine.

You may think this is a new brain child I dreamed up while washing dishes. But this technique of good gardening and lawn care has been around a long time, at least all the sixty-eight years that Grandma Putnam lived. And I'll bet you can remember your grandmother throwing the sudsy dishwater over the roses and kitchen garden. This is an old idea that will work for you.

Aeration

Next let's give your lawn a good massage. That's right, a massage. I'm not going to tell you to get down on your knees and use your fingers to rub your lawn's scalp into a nice rosy condition. But I do want you to use your feet.

There's a lot of talk today about the value of jogging. It's a great remedy for those tired winter muscles and a sluggish heart so I recommend it. Only here's how to get double mileage out of your running.

Put on a pair of spiked track shoes, baseball or golf shoes and run around your yard. The spikes do the trick. The holes punched in the soil let water, air and food down to the hungry roots. Jogging with spiked shoes also breaks up compaction, the packing down of the soil which crushes and smothers the important root system.

If you'd rather get your exercise from gardening and puttering around the yard, then put on the spikes while you're walking. At the close of the day, take an inspection tour around the lawn with your spikes on. Give a little pep talk of loving encouragement to the flowers, shrubs and vegetables. They'll talk back with soothing words of cheer that will make you sleep sweeter and enjoy life more.

What every lawn needs is aeration, which is what I've been talking about. You can also rent a machine called a lawn plugger that removes plugs of soil, or you can buy a hand plugging tool. Once a year, after de-thatching and shampooing, it's a good practice to go over your lawn with a plugging tool.

Leave the plugs of soil on the lawn and break them up with the back of a rake.

Mother Nature doesn't smooth out all the bumps in

a meadow by rolling a heavy log over them or pounding them down with a rock. She gently works over the rough spots with the rain above and earthworms, moles and gophers underground. Now I don't recommend you call in the moles and gophers to smooth your lawn. These lawn pests do more damage than good in your front yard.

I do suggest you copy Mother Nature's gentle ways. Remember the three "P's" of good lawn care. Use patience to smooth the humps and bumps. Don't go rumbling over Benny the Blade with a great heavy roller like you're ready to put in a superhighway. That's what rollers are for, to compact surfaces for reinforcement and to eliminate soil expansion. This is OK for parking lots and driveways.

If you want to smooth out some bumps, take a plugger and remove some of the extra soil. When you water the remaining soil, it will have some place to spread out.

Or if the bump is large, you might use a spade to cut around the mound, lift off a layer of sod, remove some earth and replace the turf like a cover. Gullies and tire ruts can be repaired in just the opposite manner. Lift the turf, fill with soil and replace.

On an established lawn, a heavy roller packs the soil down and shuts out water, air and nourishment. Roots suffocate when crushed by a heavy weight. For this reason it's a good idea to keep automobiles or trucks off your lawn.

Seeding a new lawn or putting down sod are the only operations that call for the use of a roller. And this should be an empty, light roller used only to press the seed into the rough ground. Using the roller over newly laid sod forces the roots to make firm contact with the earth beneath and pushes the joints and butt ends together.

I am sure that I will not win the lawn roller manufacturers' award again this year!

Mowing

Lawn cutting is the most common and taken-for-granted lawn job there is. Few people give it much thought, but there is a right time and a right way to cut. After all the work you put into proper growing practices, you don't want to defeat your purpose by sloppy mowing.

A lawn is not cut just for looks. The main reason is to increase branching or new blade growth. When there are more plant surfaces, more photosynthesis can take place, thus enabling the rhizome, or growing factory, to utilize food. This food is then changed into chlorophyll, which is sent back through the system, giving the grass a lush green color.

The second reason grass is cut is to make each blade stand tall and straight. We don't want Benny to get round shouldered, do we? That's what happens when grass is allowed to grow too tall; it bends over onto another blade. This shades the roots and makes for an overall tired, run-down feeling. You end up with everybody lying down on the job.

Another reason for regular mowing is to stimulate the flow to chlorophyll. When a blade is cut, the rhizome sends a rush of fluid up to the top to seal the fresh cut.

Since the green leaves of plants produce the food necessary for growth, you should not let the lawn grow very tall before it is cut back, leaving mostly yellowed stubble.

If you ever get to thinking that a blade of grass is a pushover, remember this. A single blade of grass forcing its way through the earth exerts the equivalent of 4,600 pounds of thrust per square inch. That's a lot of power! Better watch where you stand when you're adding that super-special plant food. You might get launched like a rocket!

To Cut
or Not to Cut,
That Is the Question

When's the best time to cut your lawn? To answer that question we need to consider what happens when grass is cut. Newly cut blades of grass are exposed to the elements of sun and wind. Secondly, the surface of the roots are exposed to these elements, which creates a situation of shock. It's like working in an air conditioned office all day and stepping out onto a July sidewalk. You know what that's like.

To modify this shock from the hot sun and dry noonday wind, I like to cut my grass in the cool, pleasant part of the evening. It's more comfortable for me, and my grass enjoys its haircut more also. The grass has time to adjust to its trimming before the sun comes up strong.

The moisture content of both the soil and grass should be taken into consideration. The barber prefers

your hair to be dry when he cuts it. Grass also cuts best when it's dry. Wet grass matted under the mower causes the blade to pull the ends off instead of giving a good clean cut.

When grass is pulled, the roots or runners get dislodged and this causes a festering condition. The rhizomes will die, leaving your lawn looking like it has the "mange." Grass will drop out like falling hair. So cut your grass when dry and give it a nice drink the next morning.

How Often to Cut

How often you cut your lawn will determine both its quality and density. The blue grasses, Merion and Kentucky, will be the greenest and healthiest if they are cut one-and-a-half to two inches every two days, and don't forget to collect the clippings. The ryes and fescues should be cut twice a week, bent grasses every other day, and dichondra once a week. That's what I said, once a week. You may have heard that dichondra can be cut only once a month—but that isn't true.

There is such a product as a growth inhibitor for lawns. But I recommend them only for commercial use. Never try to cut corners by lowering the wheels and giving your lawn a close shave. You'll ruin your grass.

Cutting Words

You may think that it doesn't matter which direction you mow. This is only partially true. Professional greens superintendents feel that for beauty and good health, a definite pattern should be followed.

First mow one or two mower widths around the outside area of your lawn. The next time you cut your lawn, begin this first strip by cutting in the opposite direction.

27

STEEP SLOPES

If your lawn has an area with a fairly steep slope you will no doubt have a problem establishing and maintaining a turf there. Mowing a sloping lawn is usually a dangerous job and even with the best equipment it is almost impossible to avoid "scalping" at the top of the rise.

And of course slopes lose moisture so fast that watering is a problem. Slopes can be planted to grass, or sodding may be used, but because of the difficulties mentioned, such areas are best planted to a ground cover, whenever possible.

*Keep your lawn mower blade sharpened and properly
adjusted for maximum mowing efficiency.*

Next cut in straight back and forth strips across
the lawn. Cut a circle around trees and flower beds and
then keep on with your normal cutting pattern until
you have finished. Each time you cut your grass, change
the direction of your mowing pattern so that the grass
won't grow in only one direction.

Don't walk on the grass where you are about to cut
or it will lie down and give an uneven cut.

I must emphasize the importance of always using a
good sharp blade. A dull blade will rip, tear and beat
the grass to death. The shattered, ragged ends of such
butchered grass will dry out and cause your lawn to take
on a poor color and lusterless appearance.

Benny the Blade says—
"You don't shave with a dull edge,
why shear me with one!"

31

Buy a new mower blade each spring. Every month change blades and have the blade you take off sharpened for its next tour of duty. A reel-type mower needs to have a smooth sharpening stone run over the blade edges before each mowing. Once a month I take it to a professional for a complete sharpening job.

The new plastic mower blades do a good job and are safer. These blades also need to be rotated and sharpened each month.

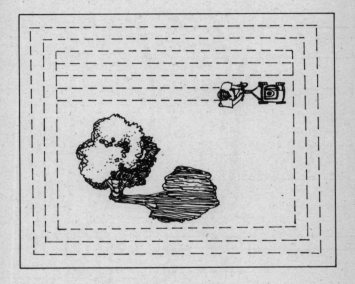

This diagram shows the cutting pattern approved by the greens superintendent of your country club. Mow two widths around the exterior of your lawn and then a normal cross-lawn cut. Be sure to alternate direction each time you mow.

Mowers

The type and quality of mower you use will make lawn care a pleasure or a drudgery. Your choice between the reel type or rotary, riding or walking is a personal choice. No one can settle an argument over which is best. But let me give my opinion. I prefer the reel type mower, as do most golf courses and sod growers.

The rotary mower will also do a fine job, but they must be kept sharp, tuned and balanced. The undercarriage must be kept clean of clippings. Keep the mower moving, as letting it stand in one position may create settling circles. Stop and start the mower on a smooth hard surface free of loose stones.

A special reel mower using seven blades must be used to cut bent grass as well as most southern and western grasses.

Let me say again for emphasis, after cutting your grass, always collect the grass clippings to avoid a thatch build-up. This is important.

The reel-type mower is preferred by lawn lovers who want to give their grass the best tender loving care. It cuts neater, cleaner and distributes the clippings evenly over the lawn.

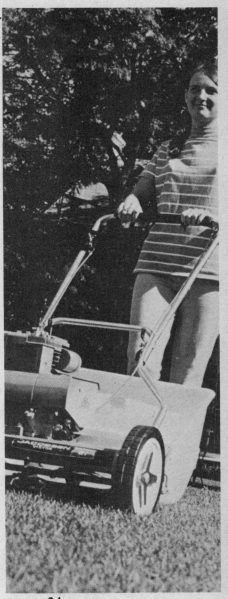

The popular rotary mower seen buzzing over most lawns in suburbia has the advantage of being inexpensive and easily maintained. The most important thing to remember is that they must be regularly sharpened— and kept sharp. You must adjust the blade for proper height according to the type of grass.

JACOBSEN

35

Watering

You can't live very long without water. Your lawn is not any different. Let Benny the Blade go too long without a good fresh drink and he will dehydrate. On the other hand, if you soak him with too much water, he'll get fat, soft and tender. In this shape, your grass is susceptible to disease and injury. You can't turn off a thunder cloud, but you can control the sprinkler. Keep your lawn tough and in fighting trim with the proper amount of water.

Your Grass Has Good Taste

All water may look alike, but don't be fooled. H_2O scientifically may have the same basic formula, but remember that rain and snow have natural trace elements that can add health to your lawn.

Rain water is the best water of all for plants. During an electrical storm, the rain particles are charged with as much as seventy-eight percent nitrogen. You can see why plants look so cheerful after a cool gentle rain.

Well water may have important trace elements, such as iron, which is important to people and plants. Well water is lower in nitrogen than rain water, though.

Water from your kitchen faucet has many trace elements, plus a lot of unwanted chemical additives. Fluoride is put in some community water to give the kids strong teeth. Chlorine is used to kill germs. Your plants have a distaste for some of these additives. One bad villain coming out of your faucet is plain old sodium salt. Too much salt isn't good for you, and it certainly doesn't do your lawn any good. In fact, many

Your grass loves good ole rain water best. Chemical additives in tap water can be harmful to your beautiful lawn.

lawns are killed by this sneaky creep hiding in your water.

The best and most pure water available runs down your rain spout and out into the sewer every time it rains. It's time to revive the old-fashioned rain barrel and have on hand a continuous supply of Mother Nature's tonic. I have one. It's great to be able to dip up a bucket of water to splash around the flower beds and know it's full of trace elements—and fertilizer. Did you know that simple rain water contains a mild but high-nitrogen fertilizer? The analysis would read 78-21-1. In the air above us, one cubic foot contains seventy-eight percent nitrogen, twenty-one percent phosphorus and one percent inert matter.

Keep It Clean

One simple way to purify our city processed water is to get yourself a gadget called a robot gardener. It was popular a few years ago and you may have one still hanging in the back of the garage. The robot gardener was a plastic apparatus into which you could put a cartridge of fertilizer or insecticide. As the cartridge dissolved, it spread the fertilizer evenly over the lawn.

Here's a new use you can make of an old tool. Get some agricultural charcoal from a garden center or variety store and fill up the plastic container part with

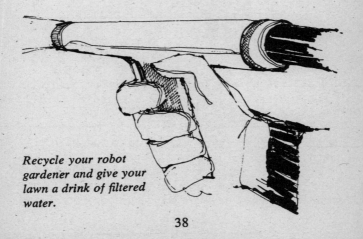

Recycle your robot gardener and give your lawn a drink of filtered water.

charcoal. As the water passes through the charcoal, it takes out much of the salt and other impurities.

If you want a small supply of pure water for your house plants, collect the water from a dehumidifier or from defrosting the refrigerator. Of course this won't

Whoa—Benny says, not so much water.

BACK-YARD LIVING

More and more people are finding pleasure in back-yard leisure
time. It's fun to eat there, to
sunbathe, or just to sit in the
sun or shade, whichever happens
to feel best. And it is especially
nice to have friends and family
gathered there. What better use
could there be for your lawn?

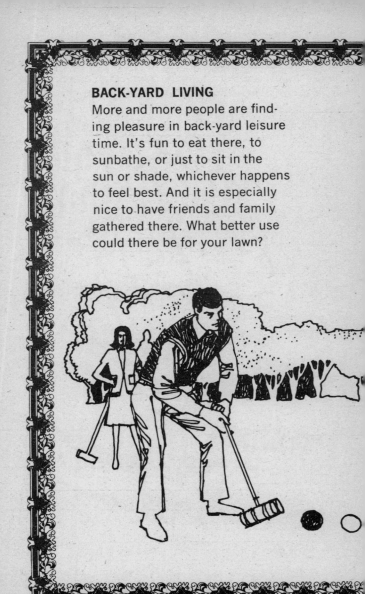

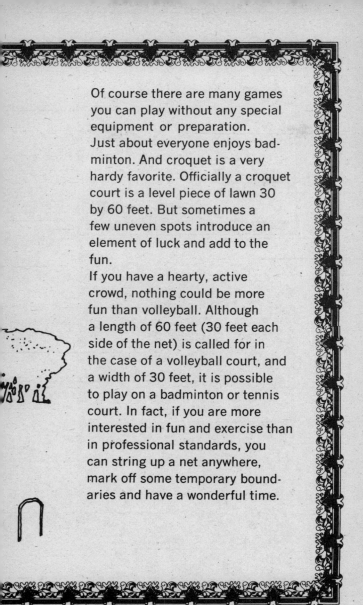

Of course there are many games
you can play without any special
equipment or preparation.
Just about everyone enjoys badminton. And croquet is a very
hardy favorite. Officially a croquet
court is a level piece of lawn 30
by 60 feet. But sometimes a
few uneven spots introduce an
element of luck and add to the
fun.

If you have a hearty, active
crowd, nothing could be more
fun than volleyball. Although
a length of 60 feet (30 feet each
side of the net) is called for in
the case of a volleyball court, and
a width of 30 feet, it is possible
to play on a badminton or tennis
court. In fact, if you are more
interested in fun and exercise than
in professional standards, you
can string up a net anywhere,
mark off some temporary bound-
aries and have a wonderful time.

HERCULES INC.

give you enough water to keep Benny the Blade and all his cousins happy, so you'll just have to depend on Jupiter Fluvius, Mother Nature's right-hand man, god of the rains.

Rise, Shine and Sprinkle

When you're depending upon a thundercloud to do the watering job, you have to be happy whenever the work gets done. But if you have a choice of times to water, the best time is in the morning, just after the sun smiles above the trees. While the dew is clinging to each blade of grass, turn the sprinklers on and give the yard a good soaking.

I know you've heard this before, but it's very important. Put enough water on your yard so it penetrates deep. If just the surface is wet, the roots will all grow near the surface to drink the water where you put it. When the hot dry days of August arrive, the soil will quickly dry out—maybe while you're on vacation. The roots will dry and your grass will burn. Shallow watering will one day leave you with a brown, dead lawn.

The reason for early morning watering is so the grass will have a chance to dry out in the hot, sunshiny part of the day. If your lawn stays wet through the cool of the night and is soggy much of the time, you'll soon be plagued with fungi and other lawn diseases. Nitrogen in the soil keeps the earth warm while the top of the grass is cool from the dew, thus creating an ideal incubation condition for disease. I admit it's a little extra trouble to water in the morning, but it's well worth the effort.

If you went to bed with wet clothes on between wet sheets and a wet mattress and left the window open, in a few nights you'd have a little fungus between your toes and behind your ears. Soon you'd begin to itch and scratch. Your grass gets the itches too, and disease soon follows.

People ask me why golf courses water all night. That's simple. People prefer to play golf in the sunshine without sprinklers dumping water in their shoes. Besides, golf courses are usually sprayed with a fungicide once or twice a week to combat fungus disease. So don't copy the watering habits of the greens superintendent, unless you're collecting greens fees.

How to Water

Watering is a simple job, but it needs to be done properly. Remember I said to water deep. Well, how deep is deep?

For the average lawn, the cool grasses, such as Merion and Kentucky blue, the ryes (which are both cool and warm), the red fescues, *Poa trivialis,* or any other cool grass: water to a depth of about three inches. For dichondra, zoysia, and Bermuda, it's a good idea to water to a depth of two inches. Even though you are in sandy soil, water deep so that the roots get used to staying down there.

How do you know when you have two, three or four inches? That's simple. Take a coffee can or a used fruit tin can and place it out at the farthest point that the water reaches. When the can is full, three or four inches, or whatever you've determined you want, stop watering. The can acts as a homemade water meter.

It's a good idea to do this at least twice a week. It isn't going to do your lawn any good if you water a little every day, because a little every day doesn't help at all. As a matter of fact, it harms, because that's shallow watering, and the lawn will react by growing shallow roots, which weakens it and makes it susceptible to all sorts of damage.

Benny says—
"*Fungus-amungus to you too pal!
How would you like to sleep in a wet
bed every night?*"

45

Sprinklers

There are many kinds of water sprinklers on the market today. As you might expect, the best is also the most expensive. This is an automatic system installed in your lawn. It comes with a water meter and a timer that turns it on at a certain time. It sprinkles for a set time period at a constant pressure, thereby watering to a depth you indicate. But this system, besides being expensive, involves tearing up the lawn; these two considerations cause most people to turn to a more simple device.

If you have the time, you might consider a do-it-yourself watering system kit available at most department stores and garden centers. These work fine, are very effective and should cost you only about one tenth of what you would pay for a professionally installed system.

Perhaps neither the first or second suggestion is suitable to your situation. Then you will probably join the multitude of home owners who use the trusty, ordinary lawn sprinkler. For getting the water delivered to the lawn fastest, I prefer a pulsator—the one that sings a little song of "chicka-chicka-chicka." The spray can be regulated to a small circle or a large one. Actually, they cover quite a large area—four of them will water approximately 5,000 square feet at a time.

The wand-type sprinklers come in a variety of styles and any of them will work fine. They are especially useful for hard-to-reach areas. There are some with adjustable heads that water in oblong, square, or circular patterns, a useful and practical feature for many lawns. However, it does take a little longer to do the job than the other systems discussed here.

Sometimes you will hear someone recommend that you give a lawn a liquid feeding as it is watered. I have never found this method advisable for amateurs. I think this is because people have a tendency to forget, or overfeed, and this burns the lawn. However, I highly recommend a hose-end sprayer for home lawn use. You know, the gadget that uses a jar fitted on the end of the hose so that liquid fertilizer can be put into it. Although this is a good way to feed the lawn, it must not be considered watering the lawn. In fact, it would be a good idea to apply fertilizer in this manner after the lawn has been watered.

Our friends from Scott lawns show you what happens with improper watering.

IDEAL SITUATION
Adequate air-pore space, with moisture at all depths. As moisture is lost it is replaced.

SATURATION
When soil becomes saturated with moisture, movement of air is blocked. Grass blades tend to become limp; the roots cease to penetrate and remain near the soil's surface.

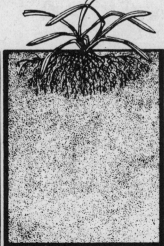

More Than Enough
Is Too Much

I use the phrase, "Grass can't swim," because I want to impress you with just how much plants, especially grass plants, are like human beings. Water is an essential part of our diet, and in order to stay in the best of

LACK OF MOISTURE
As drying out occurs, plant growth is stunted and tips turn brown. Feeder roots near the surface are first to succumb and gradually die back to lower depths. Roots thrive only at lower depth where moisture may be available.

LIGHT WATERING
Plant obtains slight, temporary relief with shallow roots absorbing moisture at the surface. This results in inadequate deep rooting so that normal surface drying leaves plant in depleted condition and can result in severe damage.

health, we have to be sure to get adequate amounts of this vital fluid. But we weren't made to breathe under water, and anyone who tries it will get into trouble. Grass also depends on oxygen, and if too much water is used and the roots are kept underwater for some time or if the grass blade is submerged, then the plant smothers. And Benny the Blade can't even yell for a lifeguard!

It's fairly common to see discolored soggy spots in a lawn because of overwatering. You'll have to be temperate, even in watering, especially if your soil is not well drained.

Clay soils can present watering problems because they are usually not well drained. Sometimes there are pockets in the ground and places where the ground is not level or has not been graded to allow the water to drain away. Grass will have a tough time under these circumstances.

Fertilizers

Because we cut our grass often, the plants never reach true maturity as, say, field grass or hay does. Since lawn grass is kept at a juvenile level, it requires a special formula, just as human babies do.

The first consideration in choosing a formula for your lawn is nitrogen. The type of nitrogen and how it will affect the growth of plant life is important. There is a relatively new organic nitrogen fertilizer called ureaform. Its chemical structure permits the nitrogen to be made available slowly and in adequate amounts for the continuous feeding of plants.

To be sure you are getting a quality lawn fertilizer, you should check the percentage of WIN (water-in-

Benny the Blade says—
"Remember my appetite—I'm a
growing boy."

soluble nitrogen). This should be at least 35% of the total nitrogen content. The higher the WIN, the better the quality of the fertilizer and the greater its safety and longevity.

Switch formulas every other time to vary the lawn's diet, or it will get bored and will not react after a while, just as you and I would get bored by a repetitive, day-in, day-out diet.

I also recommend that you begin and end each growing season with a complete feeding as prescribed by the manufacturer. In the cool parts of the country, do this just before the snow season and again just after. In the winter rainy areas, do this just before and after the rains. In the South, October and May seem to do the job, and in the dry West, October and February will fill the bill.

What pH Means to Your Lawn

pH can be loosely defined as "parts of hydrogen ions," which determine the acidity of the soil. This is a factor that greatly influences a plant's ability to use the plant food available.

For fertilizers to do their job, the pH of the soil should be between 6.0 and 7.0. Soil tests are the only sure way to keep soil conditions right and to be sure that your soil is supplying the minor nutrients needed by grass.

The three most common trace elements that all plants need are nitrogen, phosphorus and potash. The numbers on the front of most lawn food bags indicate the percentage of each of these three elements that is contained in the particular product. You need only multiply each of these numbers by the weight of the bag to find out, in weight, what you are getting for your money. In most cases we are after all the nitrogen we can get. You may be wondering what the rest of the bag is

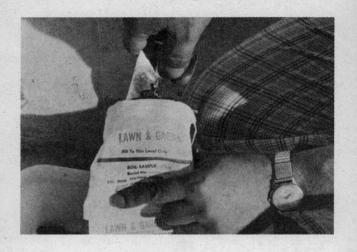

Here is a simple way to get a sample of your lawn soil for the test: Drive a small pipe into the ground. Remove it and poke out the soil with an old coat hanger. Get samples from a variety of areas in your lawn. Mix these soil samples together, bag them and send them to your local United States Department of Agriculture Experiment Station. Each state has such a station and the tests are made free or for a small sum.

You may make your own tests with a soil testing kit. The directions that come with the kit are easy to understand and easy to follow.

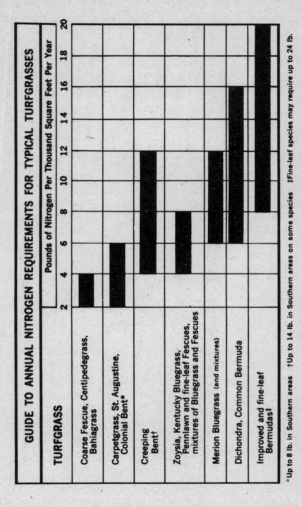

GUIDE TO ANNUAL NITROGEN REQUIREMENTS FOR TYPICAL TURFGRASSES

TURFGRASS	Pounds of Nitrogen Per Thousand Square Feet Per Year
	2 4 6 8 10 12 14 16 18 20
Coarse Fescue, Centipedegrass, Bahiagrass	████ (4)
Carpetgrass, St. Augustine, Colonial Bent*	██████ (6)
Creeping Bent†	████████████ (12)
Zoysia, Kentucky Bluegrass, Pennlawn and fine-leaf Fescues, mixtures of Bluegrass and Fescues	████████ (8)
Merion Bluegrass (and mixtures)	████████████ (12)
Dichondra, Common Bermuda	████████████████ (16)
Improved and fine-leaf Bermudas‡	████████████████████ (20)

*Up to 8 lb. in Southern areas   †Up to 14 lb. in Southern areas on some species   ‡Fine-leaf species may require up to 24 lb.

Different types of grass require varying amounts of nitrogen. Check with the chart for your lawn needs.
Notice it gives the total yearly amounts required.

54

The cartoon is funny, but you *should know what the numbers in a fertilizer analysis mean. 10-4-2 fertilizer contains 10% nitrogen, 4% phosphorus and 2% potash!*

"Frankly, I don't know what the numbers mean, unless it's the odds on the weeds winning."

full of. It is the carrier or filler that the manufacturer uses to fill up the bag so you can safely put it through your spreader.

How much should you buy? As professionals, we try to spread one pound of actual nitrogen per 1,000 square feet of lawn area each time we apply.

Here is a simple formula that you can use to determine how many bags of lawn food you will need to get one pound of nitrogen per 1,000 square feet in each application.

Multiply the length of your lot by the width, then divide by ten. Then divide *that* by the amount of nitrogen (the first number on the bag) and this will tell you exactly how many pounds to buy. Example: using a 10-6-4 lawn food on a 50' x 100' lawn: 50 x 100 =5,000 square feet ÷ 10=500 ÷ (N) 10=50 pounds. Try it with your lot and your favorite brand fertilizer formula.

Dinner on the Grounds

I have seen the oddest patterns on some lawns, because the garden buff either had a damaged spreader or poor vision, or was drunk. Do not apply lawn food if any of these is the case.

The end results will depend somewhat on the type of spreader used. If you can find a broad spreader that

Benny the Blade says— "Oh-oh, here comes that drunk."

There are many types of spreaders on the market. Pick one that fits your needs and your budget.

throws the food in a flaring pattern, I think you will soon agree this type does the best job.

To avoid the problem of odd patterns, I divide the amount of fertilizer I plan to use in half. Using the first half, I work back and forth in one direction. Then I spread the rest of the fertilizer in rows at right angles to the first. This way it's hard to skip places.

In case this section on lawn feeding seems short in view of its importance, let me reassure you—it is a short chapter because it is a simple subject. Benny the Blade is no finicky guest; treat him like one of the family.

It's always wise to check with local garden stores to see what formulas are most used in your area. Then consult with the old pocketbook and make your choice.

Weeds

Benny the Blade does have a few mortal enemies, and you might as well figure on some sneaky attacks from them. The dictionary, as usual, describes them pretty well: "weed, n. any plant growing uncultivated, useless or troublesome, offensive or hurtful." And those words go double for dandelions. Today one dandelion, tomorrow hundreds. You discover one of those fluffy, golden-headed things in your lawn one sunny morning and right on the spot you feel your green thumb fading a couple of shades.

Well, you have to relax. Too many people run into the weed battle without any strategy whatsoever. You can waste a lot of time, effort and money that way.

Weeds are not all that bad. As a matter of fact, I haven't found a weed I couldn't like. I don't always like it where I find it, but eventually we reach a mutual understanding on where we will both enjoy the other's company.

Dandelion greens are a most delicious and nutritious food—certainly they are economical. I grow, cultivate, feed and harvest two crops from the dandelion. First the greens and then the yellow flowers, which I brew into a golden nectar. So you can see this is a rather handy weed to have.

Our ancestors, wise in ways we have forgotten, found many uses for weeds. You may read fascinating items in an old Herbal. Such as the fact that plantain was used to bring bad spirits outs of a person. So you can see it might not hurt a thing to get acquainted with a few weeds here and there.

Weeds are a good sign in a way. When a sod grower or a golf course designer is looking for new land, they both look for ground covered with a good growth of weeds. This shows the soil is fertile, and they know it

will grow good grass once they have overcome the weeds with a modern herbicide (weed killer).

But when the time comes for you to make an attack on the weeds in your own lawn, you must know what you are about. It is all too easy to purchase the wrong kind of control, destroy your precious grass and leave the weeds to thrive.

Know
the Enemy

To make things simple, let's begin with the two categories of weeds Mother Nature devised just to keep you on your toes. The first is the "monocot," or grassy

Some common weeds you're bound to meet in your front yard.

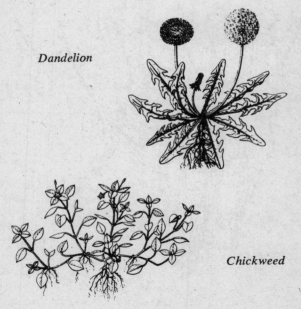

Dandelion

Chickweed

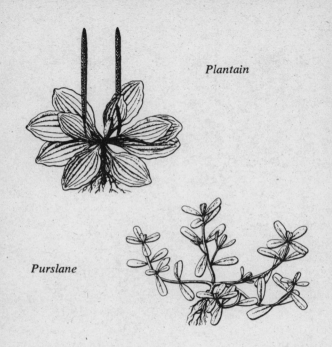

Plantain

Purslane

weed, such as goosegrass, crab grass, nut grass, foxtail, dallis grass and witch grass. These annual monocots live one full season, go to seed, then their old foliage dies forever. But the new seed sprouts a hundred-thousand-fold—which can cause one heck of an Excedrin head-ache for someone who's trying to grow a good-looking lawn.

Perennial monocots, such as tall fescues, timothy, and orchard grass will return each year from the rhizome.

Yes, and More

The second category is the "dicot," or the broad-leafed weed. In this category we find our most persistent pests. Purslane, chickweed, dandelion, henbit, oxalis,

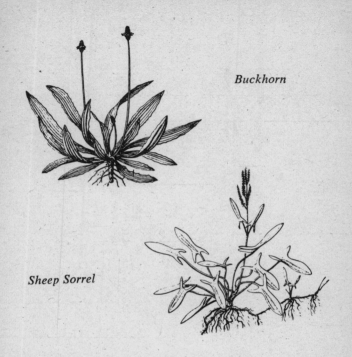

Buckhorn

Sheep Sorrel

thistle, plantain, buckhorn, clover, ground ivy and knot-weed are all dicots.

Now walk out and look at your lawn and its weedy inhabitants. Can you recognize them? What next?

When All Else Fails

Your first line of defense is a really healthy lawn. When your lawn is dethatched properly and often, shampooed, aerated, fed well, watered and mowed often, weeds are hardly any problem, and very few chemical controls are necessary. So this is the best method of control.

POWER HELPER

One aid to a neat lawn is a powerful little machine that vacuums up
clippings, litter and even leaves,
saving you the trouble of raking
them. As a bonus you have the
organic material to use in your
compost heap or as a concen-
trated mulch. Model shown
JET-AIRE Model 50040,
by Jacobsen.

But if your lawn is not at the peak of health and you have a weed problem, here are my suggestions. Broad-leaf weeds can be controlled with 2,4-D, a growth stimulator hormone that makes the plants grow themselves to death, combined with banvel, a herbicide. You will find these weed killers packaged under various brand names, and when used as directed, they are very effective.

It is best to get at the monocots, or annual grassy weeds, while they are asleep. A pre-emergence treatment will kill the seed when it is dormant, before it can germinate or sprout in the spring. Bandane is a chemical compound that may be bought under many popular brand names. I have found it safe and effective.

Not So Fast!

But beware! Not all lawns are grass, as some unsuspecting easterners have discovered when they moved west and south and met dichondra, a ground-cover substitute for grass and a member of the morning-glory family. If you use a common weed killer on this type of lawn, you can kiss it all goodbye.

When you move in and can't identify your variety of lawn, visit your local nurseryman with a sample of the turf area. It sure is better to be safe than sorry.

When to Attack

You might say the secret to successful weed control is timing. As we mentioned, the broad-leaf weeds (dicots) can be effectively destroyed by a combination of 2,4-D and banvel. This should be applied in the early spring when the weeds are thriving, not when it is hot and dry. You will find that a liquid spray seems more effective than a dry application. Although any of

"How disgraceful—me, a ground cover, nearly wiped out by a weed killer!"

REMEMBER THE CHILDREN

If there are children in your family you will want to give some special thought to their pleasure— a swing, a low treehouse, a sand-pile or box. If you can work it out, a playhouse would spread around a lot of joy. It only takes a couple of days to build one and you could make special adaptations like maybe some decking around and one side jutting out so it could double as a little theatre. Playing outdoors im-proves the appetite, sleep and disposition of children (that goes for adults, too).

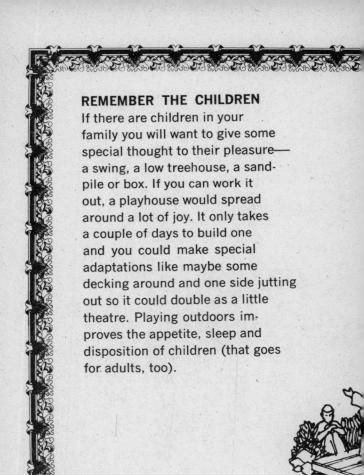

the dry weed killers will give you great results, they do usually take a little longer to do the job. And please! Try to find a still, calm day to do this work. A little wind could spread the poison, damaging nearby shrubs or flowers before you realize what is happening.

A dry weed killer can be applied with the criss-cross method described in the lawn feeding section.

Sprayers

The monocots, crab grass being the most devastating, are best controlled by applying a pre-emergence killer which contains the chemical bandane early in the spring before the evening temperatures get to fifty degrees, in a criss-cross pattern. To win this battle, you need only remember that you must concentrate on kill-

H. D. HUDSON CO.

If you have a large lawn or if you garden avidly, maybe you should invest in a power sprayer. It could save you a lot of time and effort.

If you're strictly a weekend gardener with a small or average lawn, a hand sprayer is probably adequate. Whatever your specific needs, Hudson has a sprayer to fit them.

ing the seed, not the plant (as you do in the case of the broad-leafed weeds).

This whole problem of weed control has been confused and compounded by much talk with chemical terms and big words and bigger theories.

Diseases

It doesn't hurt to consider for a moment the fact that most lawn grasses are grown under unnatural conditions. We can say this because their natural habitat is totally different from your yard in terms of soil, light and moisture conditions. Since you are attempting to grow plants where they ordinarily would not grow, you can expect one of the many fungus diseases to try and attack your lawn whenever there is an opportunity.

The best defenses against these lawn diseases are, of course, the good cultural practices that we have discussed throughout this chapter. De-thatch and shampoo regularly to destroy the destructive spores. Aerate the soil with spikes whenever you're working on the lawn. Always remove the grass clippings when mowing. Water before 2:00 p.m. to allow the grass to dry out before evening. And feed regularly.

Use of Gypsum

Garden gypsum is surely one of old Benny the Blade's best friends. It is a natural soil conditioner, it neutralizes salt, breaks up clay, catches nitrogen, prevents and repairs damage done by dog urine, firms up dry spots and neutralizes alkaline soil. There are many problems frequently thought to be lawn diseases which gypsum will solve. It even corrects fertilizer burn.

All possibilities should be considered before you attempt to treat a lawn disease. Since antibiotics used for a lawn disease are similar to those prescribed for a sick human, you will understand that cost for treatment can be quite expensive.

You expect your lawn to perform under a wide range of weather and soil conditions.

An application of garden gypsum will check many of the problems mistaken for lawn diseases.

If you have checked very carefully for insect damage, which causes spots, specks, patches and bruises, and found no evidence of insect pests, then you may as well gather up your courage and read further to find out more about your lawn's particular infection.

Diagnosis and Cure

The names, symptoms and suggested control of the following fungus diseases are designed to educate, not confuse. I am merely going to acquaint you with the time of the season you might expect one of these problems.

Brown patch: Brown patch attacks St. Augustine grass, rye, Kentucky and Merion blue, fescue, bent, and centipede grass. It occurs in humid regions during hot, wet weather. Brown patch will show up right after a heavy application of fertilizer during such weather, as it attacks new, lush growth. The grass will turn a brownish color in narrow streaks. Do not feed during these weather conditions; water early in the day. Apply Panogen Turf Fungicide as directed.

Leaf spot: This attacks Kentucky bluegrass in the early spring and fall when it is cool and damp. Reddish-brown to purplish spots appear on the leaf stem. Wash with soap and water and spray with Acti-Dione. Remove grass clippings and hold up heavy feeding until cured.

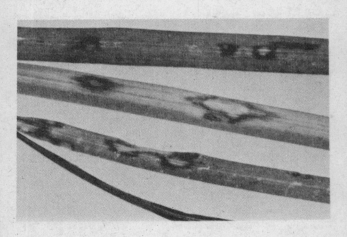

Rust: Rust attacks Merion and Kentucky bluegrass in the late summer, when heavy dew is present, and continues until frost. Reddish-brown or yellow-orange pustules develop on the leaf and stem. To control, shampoo and apply zineb. One repeat will probably be necessary.

Fading-out: This attacks fescues, Kentucky blue, Merion blue, and bent lawns. It occurs in hot, humid weather. Lawns having this disease begin to turn yellow-green, as though they need iron or a good fertilizing. De-thatch, aerate, shampoo, and spray with Acti-Dione.

Identifying
Lawn Deseases

In the case of lawn diseases, it is an absolute must to do everything possible to prevent their emergence, as the cure is costly and slow.

Dollar spot: Attacks bent grass and fescue in the humid northern part of the country, but also occurs farther south and in northern California. It occurs in the cool, wet weather and on turf that is low in nitrogen. The grass will appear to have been damaged by a dull lawn-mower blade and to be bleached out in color. When the disease is at its peak, a white web will be visible early in the morning when the dew is on the lawn. Control with soap and water and apply Acti-Dione.

Fairy rings: These occur coast-to-coast, border-to-border, and get to about all the grasses. They are enlarging rings that continue to expand two to three feet a year, with toadstools growing in the edges of the ring. To attempt control, punch lots and lots of holes eight to ten inches deep inside the circles and half the distance to the outside. Water well, apply soap and water, and spray the surface with Acti-Dione. Repeat this a week later. Repeat again and pray!

Snow mold: This disease naturally attacks the grasses of the North. Greenskeepers dread it, as it loves the bent grasses, although it also attacks most of the bluegrasses. It occurs when snow covers the turf for a long period of time, under drifts, and where poor surface drainage is present. It looks like cotton on the leaves, or a slimy, pink growth. Apply gypsum in the fall and feed heavily in October with Milorganite. Shampoo and aerate.

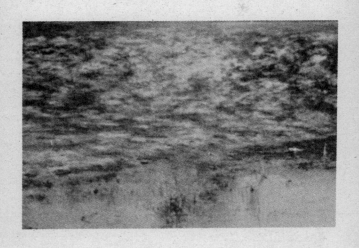

Toadstools: They will grow wherever decayed organic material is buried. Tree stumps, builders' refuse, and peat moss deposits are some of the toadstools' food supplies. To control, you should, if possible, remove the source of food. Next, punch holes eight to ten inches deep all around the area and water well. Spray with soap and water and follow with a spraying of Panogen Turf Fungicide, applied directly down the holes. At least two applications will be necessary.

ROBERT E. PARTYKA

Pests

Sometimes when you read material outlining all the diseases and problems you can encounter in a patch of grass, it makes you think about moving to the North Pole.

Hold it! Winners never quit and quitters never win. You've heard that all your life. But stop and think a minute. Have the bugs? No. As a matter of fact, bugs have precious few slogans.

The bugs probably think you grew your yard full of healthy, tender foliage as a gourmet treat for them. Why

H. ARMSTRONG ROBERTS

should a good, strong, smart bug eat old, tough dry grass and roots when he can feast on the best at your place?

Now you understand. A healthy, great-looking lawn has much appeal—even to bugs—and a neighborhood gathering on such a lawn makes good bug sense.

INSECTS

ANTS

ARMYWORMS

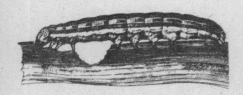

By this time you are playing around with a new thought! "I could tear up the lawn, pour concrete and paint it green." Let me hasten to reassure you, a good lawn is worth all the effort. Besides, not all these bad things will happen to your lawn—at least not at the same time!

DAMAGE	CONTROL
Annoying pests. May sting or bite. Attracted to food served outdoors.	Treat soil surface or individual mounds. Wash chlordane into soil after application.
Feed on blades of grass near soil surface.	Treat lawn surface.

CUTWORMS

CHINCH BUGS

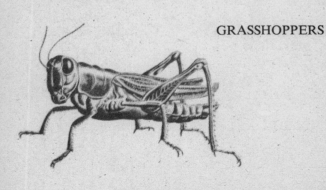

GRASSHOPPERS

DAMAGE	CONTROL
Feed on blades of grass, cutting them off at soil surface.	Treat lawn surface.
Feed on grass blades. Yellow spots appear in lawn and rapidly turn into brown, dead grass.	Mow lawn and remove thatch. Water grass thoroughly prior to applying chlordane spray. Apply chlordane spray and wash into soil surface. Repeat application within ten days and after next mowing of lawn.
Eat blades of grass.	Treat lawn surface.

ASIATIC GARDEN BEETLE LARVAE

LAWN MOTHS
(Sod Webworms)

TICKS

DAMAGE	CONTROL
Stunt or kill grass in patches, by feeding on roots.	Apply to surface of soil. Water-in thoroughly.
Fly over lawns depositing eggs, which later hatch into damaging larvae. (See Sod Webworms.)	Apply control later in the evening. Use 5-10 gallons of water per 1,000 sq. ft.
Live in lawns and attach themselves to passing humans and animals. Some species carry disease.	Treat lawn surface.

EUROPEAN CHAFER LARVAE

JAPANESE BEETLE LARVAE

MOLE CRICKETS

DAMAGE	CONTROL
Feed on roots of grass, causing patches of stunted or dead grass to appear in lawn.	Apply chlordane to soil surface and water-in to the upper two inches of soil. Heavier applications are necessary if the soil is compact and/or infestations are extremely heavy. Refer to additional information under the heading "Soil Insects."
Same as European chafer larvae.	Same as European chafer larvae.
Feed on underground portions of plants. Tunnel through the ground, leaving raised burrows on the surface of the soil.	Water lawn before application, to make mole crickets move around in soil. Then apply chlordane to soil surface.

SOD WEBWORMS

WHITE FRINGED
BEETLE LARVAE

Give the Bugs a Soapy Mouth Wash

The basic good cultural practices must be adhered to through good times and bad: De-thatch, aerate, mow, water and shampoo.

The old punishment of washing the mouth out with soap is one you will find very effective on insects. Soap has a taste they don't find appealing in any way, shape or form. Regular shampooing with a mild detergent not

DAMAGE	CONTROL
Feed on grass blades. May cut grass and pull it down into their burrows in the soil. Damage results in uneven grass, dying back of new shoots, and irregular brown spots.	Water lawn thoroughly before treatment. Apply chlordane to soil surface. Do not water again for several days.
Feed on grass roots. Result in brown, dead patches of grass.	Apply chlordane to soil and water-in thoroughly.

only drives the bugs away but also discourages their return.

I have told you how much I value Grand Prize Lawn and Garden Gypsum. When you apply this "Hadacol" of the garden kingdom, you are protecting your lawn further against insect pests. The natural sulphur contained in this substance acts as a preventative soil insecticide in the spring and fall.

Wherever you live, whatever your lawn type or conditions, you may use gypsum and soap as safe preventative insecticides without fear of changing the environment.

STORING MATERIALS

Not many materials need to be kept on hand. Fertilizer should be stored in a very dry place. Wooden or metal containers are best. Paper bags often absorb moisture, split open and spill the contents.

Peat moss can be stored in the open. Rain will only keep it moist, ready for mixing top-dressing or for patching jobs.

It is good to keep a small amount of grass seed around, so that worn spots or patches may be immediately reseeded. You can't keep a lot, however, because after a year or so, germination decreases rapidly.

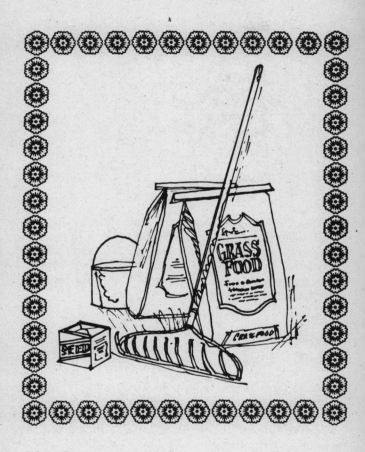

Soon the bugs will ruin your reputation for being a good host throughout the insect kingdom, by saying you are a grower of bitter foliage. It doesn't matter where you live or what kind of lawn you have, gypsum and soap will act as safe preventative insecticides without changing the environment.

Find Out
What's Bugging You

From time to time I have found it necessary to use a chemical control. When things come to that stage, I feel the problem should be handled sensibly. The exact nature of the problem needs to be determined and the offending insect identified. You may get a lot of advice from onlookers who once had a spot "just like that one," and it turned out to be such and such an insect. Don't treat haphazardly, especially where chemicals are concerned.

Get to work on your problems as soon as you can. If some doubt about identification lingers in your mind, capture a specimen in a jar and take it to your local nurseryman or to someone else who is knowledgeable and get his opinion. Ask advice about a chemical to use. Then do read every bit of the label. Buy only what you will need for the present application. Don't take the risk of storing something so dangerous for future use. You will want to follow the manufacturer's instructions to the letter. You're quite careful how you handle prescription medicine, I'm sure. In the plant kingdom the same caution is required.

When in doubt, ask for help in identifying an insect pest.

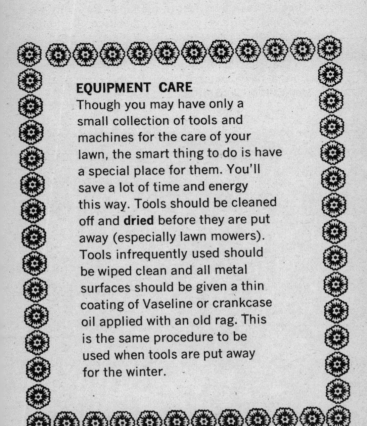

EQUIPMENT CARE

Though you may have only a small collection of tools and machines for the care of your lawn, the smart thing to do is have a special place for them. You'll save a lot of time and energy this way. Tools should be cleaned off and **dried** before they are put away (especially lawn mowers). Tools infrequently used should be wiped clean and all metal surfaces should be given a thin coating of Vaseline or crankcase oil applied with an old rag. This is the same procedure to be used when tools are put away for the winter.

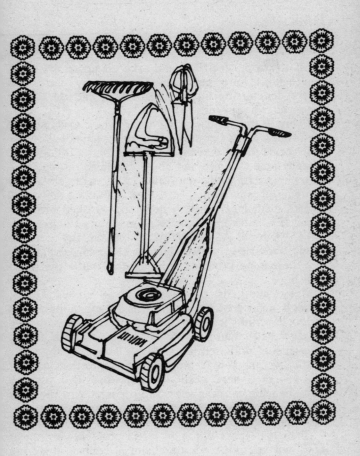

Don't Call Me

Many people feel I should take an aggressive position against hard pesticides. I get many cards and letters denouncing me for advocating the use of any chemicals whatsoever.

Every season brings to my door a new avalanche of pre-printed cards berating the hard insecticides.

It seems to me that there is more than a little inconsistency here. We use and abuse medicine on ourselves and our loved ones, man and beast, without second thoughts. I am speaking of both patented and prescribed medicines. Their benefits are extolled in newspaper, TV and radio advertisements almost constantly. Take "Aspirin A," or drink "Solution B," or take "Zap" and sleep. No wonder our children get the idea that there is no problem or discomfort that a pill won't banish.

Many hundreds of people are killed each year through misuse of these products. Many popular hot and cold drinks contain poisons that unquestionably damage the human body. Why isolate DDT for attack, when it has increased the yield per acre over the years so that we are now feeding millions more than before? The so-called hard pesticides have provided us with many benefits over the years. Before we throw the baby out with the bath water, let's see if we can't find a sensible approach to pesticides.

Chemical types: When an insect problem gets out of hand and you must rely on chemical control, there are two types to choose from. The first is a contact killer, which paralyzes the insect on contact. The second is a stomach poison, and this he must eat.

I use chlordane as recommended for soil insects, such as grubs. I use a combination spray containing pyrethrum and malathion to control the lawn moth and flying, crawling bugs and beetles on and around my lawn.

Ants are best controlled with chlordane when gypsum and soap solutions fail.

Choose your weapons: two ways to zap your insect enemy.

Bug Off!
(In Seven Steps)

When I discover that insects have launched a full-scale invasion on a lawn, I follow these steps:

1. I de-thatch. I remove all the thatch in the insect-infested area and for the same distance in the area surrounding it.

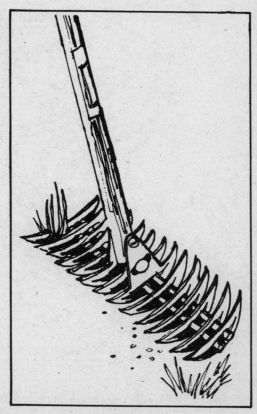

2. I aerate this area. I walk over it with cleated golf shoes and punch holes in the sod with a sharp-pointed stick or a similar object.

2

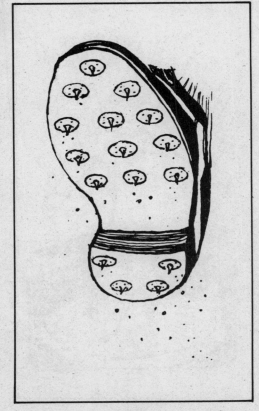

3. I water the area lightly, taking care to cover every square inch.

3

4. I shampoo with biodegradable dishwashing liquid.

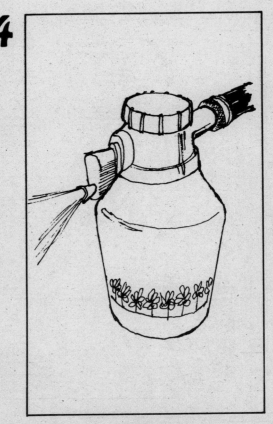

5. I apply the chemical prescribed for the particular insect problem according to the manufacturer's directions on the label.

5

6. Immediately after treating the area with chemicals, I cover it with cheesecloth or a similar thin mesh material to keep pets and birds out of the area.

6

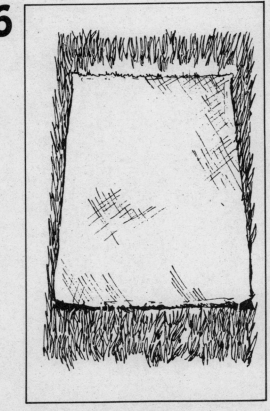

7. Cheesecloth won't keep children (or adults, for that matter) out of the treated area, so I explain the dangers to them and do my best to make them heed my warning.

The last two steps may seem overly cautious to you, but remember that they're for the protection of the lawn as well as people and animals. The grass plants have been made weak and sick by insects, so you should protect them from too many visitors while they recuperate.

New Lawn

You've finally made it. You've bought the house you and your family have been dreaming of all these years, you've packed up all your belongings, and you've moved in. You're bursting with pride at owning your own little piece of land, so you walk out the front door to survey the estate and realize your lawn looks at lot like the sand trap on your favorite golf course.

So what do you do? Chances are you have writer's cramp from writing so many checks during the last few weeks. Your savings have probably dwindled considerably—if you're lucky you'll be able to buy the week's groceries with what's left, unless the prices go up again. I don't have to tell you how expensive it is to move into a new home. You know! You've made a whopping down payment, paid a mysteriously-arrived-at amount politely called a "closing cost," and paid for gas, water, phone and electric hook-ups, plus all those miscellaneous little expenses you hadn't counted on. But you'd still like to turn your yard into a place you can be proud of. You'd like to go right out and buy all the evergreens, shrubs, trees and flowers you know you need, but you can't afford all that. So you decide to start with the lawn. You figure a lush, green lawn will do a lot for your status in the neighborhood. So how do you start?

Don't spare efforts when you are beginning your lawn. Remember a lawn will be with you throughout the years, forming a setting for all your permanent plantings.

HERCULES INC.

You take a shovel and a deep breath and start digging. After a few shovelfuls you start grumbling; after a few more you start swearing. Your building contractor, who has by now vanished into thin air, must have been playing pirate. You can tell by all the buried treasure you're finding a few inches below the surface of your "graded" lawn. Tin cans, pop bottles, leftover bricks, nails and old lumber—you've found them all. By this time you're probably so furious you can't decide whether to dump everything into the crevass the builder called "a little rut" or to crate it all up and mail it back to Captain Hook postage due.

You know you want a beautiful lawn, and grumbling and complaining never yet caused grass to grow. After you've blown off a little steam, you're going to have to cool off and get to work. You won't be alone. Mother Nature and I will be right there to give you a little advice along the way.

In spite·of what you may have been told by armchair lawn experts, you can grow a lovely green carpet of grass on any kind of soil unless there is a toxic chemical present. The soil in your yard may be saturated with oil, gasoline or salt if it was brought in

from a construction site where there was a chemical overflow. It's not difficult to detect the presence of chemicals—just smell handfuls of soil from several locations in your yard. If you notice any suspicious odors, take samples of soil to your nurseyman and ask his advice, or send the samples to a soil-testing laboratory. If the soil is sterile (which means that nothing will grow in it) because of the chemicals present, don't waste any time feeling sorry for yourself. Call your lawyer immediately. This little piece of advice could save you a lot of wasted time and money.

Pick Up Sticks

Once you're sure that your soil is not sterile, you can get on with the work ahead of you. Your first task is to pick up all the litter that's lying about. You'll

Benny the Blade says—
"I can't move (much less grow).
He's got me covered!"

116

probably find enough leftover building materials to start your own contracting business, but don't get discouraged. Pick up everything you see and dig out anything that's half buried. Don't neglect anything.

When you're sure you've picked up every nail and splinter in sight, call your children or some of the children in the neighborhood and offer a dollar to the one who picks up the most junk. You'll be surprised at how much you missed.

How to Strike Pay Dirt

Next you should spread Grand Prize Garden Gypsum over the soil surface. Apply it at a rate of fifty pounds of gypsum per 1,000 square feet of soil. This treatment is excellent for any type of soil, loam, clay or sand.

If you live in snow country, apply one hundred pounds of peat moss to every 1,000 square feet of soil. If you live in the South, the Southwest or the West, you can apply steer manure, leaf mold or partially decomposed sawdust at the same rate. The final step is to apply fifty pounds of any good-quality commercial garden food with a low nitrogen content. I usually use 4-12-4 or 5-10-5. Either one will give you what you want—beautiful, healthy grass with a strong root system. What you don't want is a big burst of growth, and this is the reason for using a low-nitrogen fertilizer.

Next you're going to have to rent a power tiller to loosen the soil and work in the material you've spread on top. Renting a tiller is not cheap, but it will allow you to get the maximum benefit from your soil additives and fertilizer, and it will save you hours of backbreaking labor.

The gypsum, fertilizer and other additives should be thoroughly mixed in to a depth of six to ten inches, and the soil should be made as fine as possible. To do so, till back and forth across the yard, then crisscross it.

117

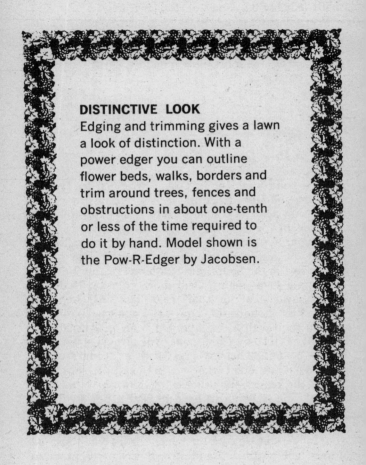

DISTINCTIVE LOOK

Edging and trimming gives a lawn a look of distinction. With a power edger you can outline flower beds, walks, borders and trim around trees, fences and obstructions in about one-tenth or less of the time required to do it by hand. Model shown is the Pow-R-Edger by Jacobsen.

Next, till from corner to corner; then crisscross that area also. If this sounds like too much work, think for a moment about how hard you'd have to work with hand tools to accomplish the same end result.

Before going on to the next step, I want to remind you to take the tiller back now. The rent for letting it sit idle in the garage is the same as it is for using it. (This little piece of advice just may save you several times the price of this book.)

It's now time to take your shovel in hand and get to work on your grade. To force runoff and to allow proper drainage, spade up the soil around the foundations of the house, the sidewalks, the driveway and all flower beds and trees.

Hills and valleys are lovely, but not in your yard. Use your shovel to shave down high spots and to fill in pockets.

Making the Grade

Getting a good grade in school took a lot of work. Getting a good grade in your lawn is no different. All I can do to help is give you a hint to make your home-work easier. Scavenge an old bed spring from a junk

GRANT HEILMAN

Your front yard is no place for "buried treasure."

A prize winning lawn begins with proper grading and smoothing.

Benny the Blade says—
*"I don't like to stand in water so
be sure to grade properly for
drainage."*

dealer, your relatives, or the city dump. Tie a rope to the front of the springs, just as you would on a sled. Leave the rope long enough to allow you to put it around your waist and drag the springs behind you. (If the rope isn't long enough, the springs will smash into your heels every time you take a step.)

Now get into your "harness" and walk in a large circle. When you've walked once around, start the second circle inside the first and walk so that the dragged areas overlap slightly. Continue this process until you're satisfied with the grade. The lawn should look smooth and level, and the grade should run away from buildings, sidewalks, drives, trees and flower beds.

To finish the job properly, take your rake and, starting from the buildings and other permanent fixtures, rake all stones, sticks and clods to the lowest point on your property.

Seed

You're finally ready to sow your grass seed. If it's late August or early September when you want to plant, you can skip soaking or refrigerating your seed if you like. (I always do it anyway just for good measure, no matter when I want to sow.) About a week before I want to plant, I put my seeds in the refrigerator and forget about them. Then when planting day arrives, I dry the seeds just enough to make them separate easily so they'll be easier to handle. The grass seed chart I've included will tell you how much you need to use on your yard.

I always hand broadcast my seeds because I think this method gives the best coverage. First I throw some small pieces of paper into the air to determine the wind direction. There's no sense fighting the wind when you can let it help you.

I stand with my back to the wind and start backing across the yard, scattering the seed as I go. Once I've covered the yard this way, I turn my side to the wind and re-broadcast over the same area, moving backward as before. Crisscrossing the area in this way insures complete coverage.

When I've finished sowing the entire yard, I cover the seed lightly with the back of my bow rake. This protects the seed from the wind and hungry birds.

Next I roll the area with an empty roller to make sure the seeds are in contact with the soil. Remember I said an empty roller. If you use a full one, you'll pack down the soil and sabotage all your plans for a beautiful lawn even before the seeds sprout.

You have just one thing left to do now, and it's one of the most important—watering. If you want your newly seeded yard to live up to its potential, you must keep it moist at all times. I said moist, not soaked. Never soak or drench the area, or your seed will end up at the

I prefer hand broadcasting of seed but you may want to try your spreader or a hand seeder.

The back of a bow rake will cover the seed enough to give contact with the soil.

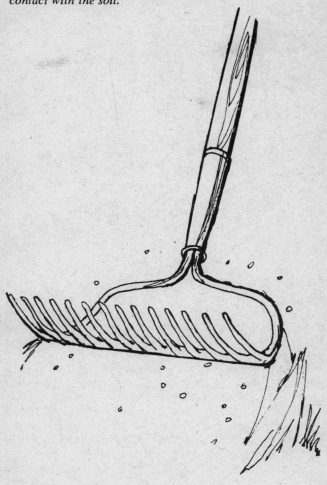

Sam Seed says—
"Roll over me lightly boys."

bottom of the grade. If the weather turns warm or windy, you may have to sprinkle several times a day.

When the young blades are one and one-half to two inches tall, you should begin your cutting program. Always use a sharp mower blade set at a height of one and one-half inches.

After four haircuts, your lawn should be fed. Give it a light, non-burning, balanced lawn food, and from then on, maintain a normal lawn feeding program.

When I'm planting sprigs, stolons or small plants, I always dip the roots in water before I put them in the ground. This seems to get the youngsters off to a better start. I've also discovered that it's better to plant the warm grasses in random patterns than in straight lines. When buying stolons, I always buy about twenty-five percent more than is recommended. I water, mow and feed a stolon-planted lawn exactly the same way as a seeded lawn.

Pick
a Winner

A lot of people choose grass seed the same way they choose a horse at the racetrack. They find a name they like and plant. If you've ever used this system at the track or on your own turf, you've learned the hard way that it doesn't pay.

You can always find someone eager to give you a hot tip on the best seed to buy, just as you can always find a "tout" to clue you in on the horses. In both places this advice usually proves to be very costly.

It's easy to recognize a lawn-seed tout. He'll have a bag of rocket-powered grass seed that he'll let you take off his hands for next to nothing—or so he says. He'll tell you the seeds are so powerful that you'd better not spill any in your car unless you want a mobile putting

*Super evergrow, evergreen seed
may not be a super bargain.*

Grass is a long-time investment. Buy your seed from a dependable source.

green. But after you've hurried home and seeded your lawn, then rushed out every morning for several weeks to check for that first sprig of green, you realize your lawn still looks like a sand trap.

Never gamble on grass seeds of unknown parentage. Buy thoroughbreds only. Check on the performance records of various seeds in your area. Find out which one ends up in the winner's circle after every race and put your money on that one. You'll come up with a winner every time.

You also need to know what type of soil you have, how well it drains and how much sun or shade your grass will get. All these factors should influence your decision.

Once you know what you want, you're ready to go out and buy your seed. Do not be hustled into buying seed from drug stores, gas stations, dime stores or other places that don't normally sell grass seed. These merchants may be honest and well-intentioned, but the odds are they don't know beans about grass seed. If you buy from them, you may end up with the wrong variety, or old or weed-infested seed.

Go to a garden center or to the gardening section of a reputable merchant. Either place should have an expert buying for them.

Always read the label on the bag or seed bin. It will give you the seed's germination record and its "bloodlines." With an inside tip like this, you can't lose.

What's in the Bag?

Germination: The percentage figure indicates what percent of the seeds in the bag will sprout. You want as close to one hundred percent as possible.

Purity: This tells you what percent of the seed is true to its name. Again, get as close to one hundred percent as possible.

Other grasses: This can be a real problem if you get the wrong grasses, especially tall fescue. Here you want as close to zero percent as possible. Then comes the big, bad wolf—weed-count. Be careful and again get as close to zero percent as possible. And lastly, inert material: this is chaff and shells.

Not all lawns are started from seed. Some begin as plugs of grass, sprigs or runners. Bermuda grass, some of the bents, St. Augustine grass and zoysia are planted from small plants and sprigs.

Dichondra, which is used as a lawn in California, is not a grass, but rather a ground cover, akin to the morning-glory. It can be grown from seed or plugs. Dichondra is reasonably easy to take care of but can keep you hopping if cut worms get a foothold.

When seeding a new lawn, I highly recommend that you use as high a percentage as possible of the permanent variety you have selected. I do not recommend that you buy a premixed blend. I would rather you do the mixing yourself. The same holds true when reseeding an old lawn. In the case of overseeding an established lawn, it is important that you use only the variety that you are trying to match up: Kentucky blue to Kentucky blue, Merion to Merion, Windsor to Windsor, and so on.

When overseeding in the Southwest, some of the South and Southern California, you will use an annual grass and not a blend. For instance, use only NK-100 rye straight, no combination.

REGIONS OF GRASS ADAPTATION

Climatic regions of the U.S. in which the following grasses are suitable for lawns: Region 1. Common Kentucky bluegrass, Merion Kentucky bluegrass, red fescue, and Colonial bentgrass. Tall fescue, bermudagrass, and zoysiagrass in southern portion of the region. Region 2. Bermudagrass and zoysiagrass. Centipedegrass, carpetgrass, and St. Augustinegrass in southern portion of the region with tall fescue and Kentucky bluegrass in some northern areas. Region 3. St. Augustinegrass, bermudagrass, zoysiagrass, carpetgrass, and bahiagrass. Region 4. Nonirrigated areas: Crested wheatgrass, buffalograss, and blue gramagrass. Irrigated areas: Kentucky bluegrass and red fescue. Region 5. Nonirrigated areas: Crested wheatgrass. Irrigated areas: Kentucky bluegrass and red fescue. Region 6. Colonial bentgrass and Kentucky bluegrass.

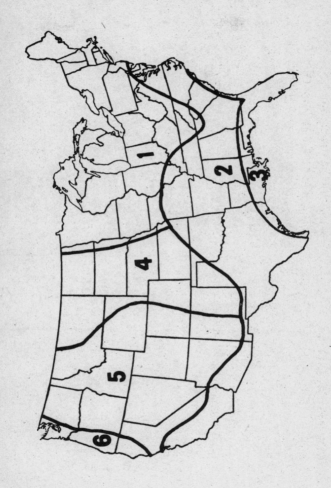

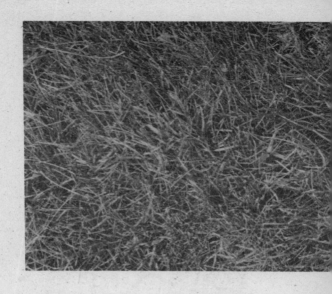

COMMON LAWN
GRASS SEEDS

Kentucky Bluegrass
(*Poa pratensis*)

Merion Bluegrass
(*Poa pratensis*)

Rough Stalk Meadow
(*Poa trivialis*)

Chewings Fescue
(*Festuca rubra,* var. *fallax*)

RATE 1000 FEET	TONE OF GREEN	LOCATION AND USE
2 lbs.	Medium	Sunny, will tolerate slight shade. Medium texture.
1 lb.	Dark	Sunny, will tolerate slight shade. Medium texture.
2 lbs.	Light	Wet, shade. Shiny leaf.
3 lbs.	Medium	Dry, shade and poor sandy soil. Fine texture.

COMMON LAWN GRASS SEEDS

Creeping Red Fescue
(*Festuca rubra*)

Highland Bent
(*Agrostis tenuis*)

Tall Fescue
(*Festuca elatior*)

Astoria Bent
(*Agrostis tenuis*)

Seaside Creeping Bent
(*Agrostis maritima*)

Penncross Creeping Bent
(*Agrostis palustris*)

Red Top
(*Agrostis alba*)

Annual Rye Grass
(*Lolium multiflorum*)

Perennial Rye Grass
(*Lolium perenne*)

RATE 1000 FEET	TONE OF GREEN	LOCATION AND USE
3 lbs.	Medium	Sandy soil. Fine texture.
½-1 lb.	Dark	Sun and light shade. Fine texture.
6-10 lbs.	Light	Athletic fields, etc. Coarse, striated leaf.
½-1 lb.	Bright	Sun and light shade. Fine texture.
½-1 lb.	Medium	Sun and light shade. Fine texture.
½-1 lb.	Dark	Sun and light shade. Fine texture.
1-1½ lbs.	Medium	Used in mixtures. Medium texture.
3-4 lbs.	Medium	Temporary lawns and in mixtures. Coarse texture.
3-4 lbs.	Dark	Temporary lawns and in mixtures. Coarse, shiny leaf.

COMMON LAWN
PLANTED PLUGS

Bermuda

St. Augustine

Zoysia

RATE PER FOOT	TONE OF GREEN	LOCATION
1 sprig	Medium	Sun and dry. Coarse texture.
1 plug	Medium	Sun and dry. Coarse texture.
1 plug	Medium	Sun and dry. Coarse texture.

Now for the bad news. Even if you buy top-quality, pure grass seed, sow it on beautifully prepared, rich soil, and water and fertilize it regularly, you may never see a single blade of grass.

Grass, like thoroughbred race horses, can be very temperamental. It has a mind of its own, and no amount of pampering will convince it to grow when it doesn't

142

want to. However, from August 15 to September 20 (give or take a few days), grass is usually very agreeable about growing. And I can see why. The harvest moon is just beginning. The evenings are beginning to get cool and invigorating, and the air is dewy. The stars are all in the right places and Mother Nature is feeling bountiful. No wonder grass likes to save its best performance until this season!

Race horses can be fooled, so can people, and so can grass. How do you fool a horse? You put blinders on him, then you can lead him anywhere. You know how easy it is to fool people—and how easy it is for them to fool themselves. If you want to plant grass seed at some time other than from August 15 to September 20, you can fool it into thinking it is time to grow.

Grandma Putnam Trick

To fool grass, mix two tablespoons of tea (not leaves) with one cup of water. Pour this mixture over the seed, using one cup per pound of seed. Mix all this together, put it in a closed container and leave it in your refrigerator for five days.

After the time is up, spread the seeds over your garage or basement floor and allow it to partially dry. Then sweep it up, being careful to get all the seed, but no nails, screws or grease. Don't worry about any dirt you pick up—it'll make spreading easier and your basement floor will be clean.

Congratulations! You've just accomplished two very clever feats. You've fooled your grass seeds into thinking it's their favorite time of year and you've fooled someone (yourself?) into sweeping your basement, which in my family is never easy to do. There are easier ways to dry damp seed, but that's our secret.

Ours and Grandma Putnam's, that is. This was one of her favorite Honey-do tricks. Honey do this and Honey do that, she'd always say. And she was so sweet and sensible, who could refuse her?

143

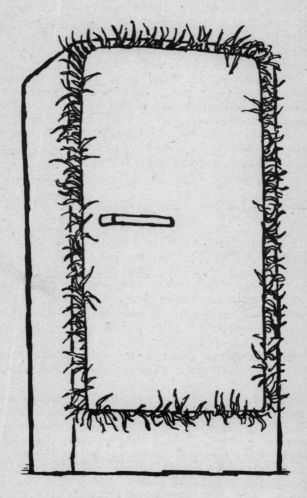

Don't take too long a vacation.

Face Lifting
for an
Older Lawn

If a lawn isn't cared for properly, it will eventually start to show its age, just as a person would. If your lawn has lost its youthful glamour, or if you've just moved into a new home with an old yard, don't despair. You can administer a miracle rejuvenation treatment that will soon return a youthful blush to your lawn's fading complexion.

I always try to schedule lawn rejuvenations for the fall, sometime in September after the children have returned to school. Your new lawn will have a much better chance of success without dozens of pairs of little feet pounding over it every day.

First, refrigerate your seed according to the directions in the seed-selection section of this book.

Your next step is to rent a power renovator or, if you prefer and can afford it, buy a roto-rake bar that will convert your rotary lawn mower into a de-thatcher. Using the criss-cross method I described earlier, go over your whole lawn. After power raking, you should rake aside all the thatch that's been brought to the surface; then repeat the whole process once more.

After de-thatching, spread fifty pounds of gypsum over every 2,000 square feet. Follow this treatment with an application of low-nitrogen lawn food, such as Winter Green or Winter Survival. Follow the manufacturer's instructions carefully.

The directions for overseeding a rebuilt lawn are the same as for a new lawn. Just remember to refrigerate your seed for about a week before you want to plant.

When you've finished overseeding, top dress the oversown area with a mixture of half soil and half peat. Now mix one ounce of Palmolive Green dish soap into ten gallons of water. Lightly water down the area with this solution, using 10 gallons per 2,000 square feet.

Don't despair if your present lawn is tired and worn out. Overseeding may be the answer.

This treatment keeps the top dressing from becoming compacted and insures good penetration.

New grass should be mown when it is two inches tall. Always remove the clippings after mowing. Maintain a regular mowing program until the grass stops growing.

You probably have problems with crabgrass no matter what part of the country you live in. If you live in the North, you can start your war on crabgrass in early March. If you live in the West or South, you can launch your attack in February. Ask your local lawn expert which pre-emergence chemical is best for use in your area.

Start your lawn program in the spring and stick to it. Your efforts will be well rewarded.

Use a mild bio-degradable soap like Palmolive dishwashing liquid for lawn shampooing. One ounce soap to ten gallons of water.

Overseeding

Gramonologists can't seem to agree as to whether you should introduce new grass into an existing lawn or not. Those who advocate doing so say the lawn will eventually grow weak from inbreeding if you don't occasionally bring in some new blood. The opponents of overseeding warn that you risk introducing diseases along with the new seed.

Personally, I think grass plants are just like people —they need a change of company every so often to keep them from getting bored. If you had to see the same people every day of your life, you'd soon run out of things to talk about and get pretty sick of always seeing the same old faces. Your grass plants are no different. Give them new neighbors and everybody will feel better.

Throw a Coming Out Party

When you overseed, you bring in exotic strangers from other areas with new stories to tell and fresh enthusiasm for growing. They'll perk up your old, jaded plants in no time.

Grass plants have romantic interests too, and overseeding gives each of your plants a chance to meet a tall dark stranger across a crowded lawn. You didn't think grass seedlings just happened, did you? I'll admit they do sometimes arrive by stork—or by robin, pigeon, crow and most other birds. The babies that do arrive this way are very likely to be illegitimate—crabgrass, quack grass and other weeds, that is. You'd be much better off to pick your lawn's friends yourself. That way

you can be sure of having offspring you can be proud of.

It's best to overseed during the same period I recommended for new seeding earlier: August 15 to September 20 in snow country and August 15 to October 15 in the West, South and Southwest. Refrigerate exactly as you did for new seed.

When overseeding the cool grasses, you should follow the rules below:

1. First you should de-thatch, using a lawn groom rake if your lawn is small. If your lawn is relatively large, you should use a roto-rake bar on your lawn mower or rent a power rake.

2. Hand sow the seed. Use half the amount recommended on the seed chart. If you want to beef up an existing stand of grass, use the same variety. Overseed Merion with Merion, for example. Don't use a mix or blend. Do use the purest, best-quality seed you can buy. Don't settle for a bargain brand.

If you have a Heinz-57 lawn—a little bit of everything—then it's OK to buy a blend, but you should still try to get top-quality seed. Pay special attention to the germination percentage.

Overseeding with Bermuda or any of the other warm grasses used for winter color requires refrigeration just as other grasses do. Never buy anything but the very best rye grass seed available. I especially like NK-100.

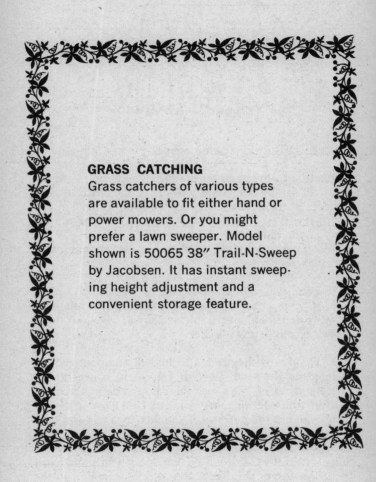

GRASS CATCHING

Grass catchers of various types
are available to fit either hand or
power mowers. Or you might
prefer a lawn sweeper. Model
shown is 50065 38″ Trail-N-Sweep
by Jacobsen. It has instant sweeping height adjustment and a
convenient storage feature.

Dichondra lawns should be overseeded once a year to keep the color bright and to replace any plants that die out.

3. If the lawn is looking sparse, top dress it with a mixture of half garden soil and half peat moss. Spread a thin layer of this mixture over the area. One-eighth of an inch should be sufficient.

4. Apply a low-nitrogen fertilizer. Winter Green and Winter Guard are among the ones you might try.

5. Water thoroughly, but don't soak. Until the new grass sprouts (in about a week) it's best to just dampen the soil in the early morning. After the grass has sprouted, resume watering as you usually do.

6. The lawn should be mowed just before you over-seed, then not again for at least seven days. When you do mow, pick up the clippings.

If you've heard that a lawn can get too thick, I suggest you ask a golf course superintendent his opinion on this issue. He'll tell you "too-thick grass" is one problem he'd love to have.

Sodding

In the last few years, the pre-grown lawn business has grown into a billion-dollar business. This affluent generation, seeming to want instant results in everything, rushes out and buys sod because it seems like the answer to an instant, trouble-free lawn. I am by no means criticizing this attitude, if you can afford it, but I do find fault with a great number of new homeowners who go to the expense of having a full-grown, mature landscape job done on their new homes. They begin with sod and end by planting fifteen- to twenty-foot trees. Then, they let the whole works become diseased or die because they don't know how to take care of their "instant landscape" after they get it.

If you truly want to get involved with the good earth, preserve what we have, and build to repair and replenish what we have abused and neglected in the past, then I will go along with anything that you wish to do in gardening. But to think that something like sod comes to you as a full-grown adult and can take care of itself —*that* grinds me no end.

Sod is the flesh of the earth and is comparable to a skin graft. Before the plastic surgeon applies a skin graft to the human body, he removes the old and dead flesh. He repairs any other damage and makes any structural changes that are needed. Then he takes patches of flesh from another part of the body, similar to the area which needs repairs, and grafts them. This bit of information is necessary so that you might better understand the points I am going to make in reference to laying sod.

If you are planning to lay sod instead of sow seed, then you must make up your mind what kind of grass you want.

When you order sod, don't try to cut corners on quality.

If your lawn is to be covered with sod, give it the same preparation required for seeding.

There are many kinds and mixes available from border to border and coast to coast. Kentucky and Merion blue, Windsor, fescue sods, field sods for road construction, bent sod and mixed sod.

The prices will vary in most locations and for various reasons. Oh yes, you can be had, the same as with seed.

Here are a couple of ways they can get you. In a new sub-division, a truck will pull up, or a man dressed in work clothes will knock on your door and say that they are just finishing up a big apartment complex and have some good sod left over, and he will sod your lot for only sixty-five cents a roll, including labor. Now let me tell you, McGee, that ain't a bad deal in anybody's book, but you don't have the lot graded.

Well, the man has his equipment there, so for twenty-five dollars he will grade it for you. Oh what a deal! For whom? Here is what you get. Ten minutes later, the tractor arrives, drops the grading blade and levels off the lawn. They don't pick up the junk, they just push it around until it falls into a rut somewhere. They don't build up your grade away from the house, trees, buildings and drives. They don't add compost, feed or soil conditioners to the weak soil for good rooting action.

Next the truck arrives with about four helpers and the driver, and they begin to unroll and unload the sod so fast that you get dizzy just watching; but you can't smell a rat yet, eh?

It's a Sod, Sod Story

What they are or could be laying in your yard is a buyout. This is a stand of sod that may, for instance, have been grown on a peat or muck bog where a weed infestation occurred. In order to control that kind of infestation, they would have had to destroy the sod. So the grower offered it for some ridiculous price, from a nickel to fifteen cents a roll, and the buyer had to cut and load it himself. The grower also stays close by when it is being cut to make sure that the buyer doesn't cut too much top soil with the sod. So you are getting a thinly cut, weed-infected turf that is not worth the powder to blow it to H**.

The men end up by sweeping the walk, turning on your sprinklers, and telling you to keep it wet.

You pay the dough by cash or check and feel great. In the meantime, the operator goes to your bank to cash your check.

Here is what you end up with. Because of the poor

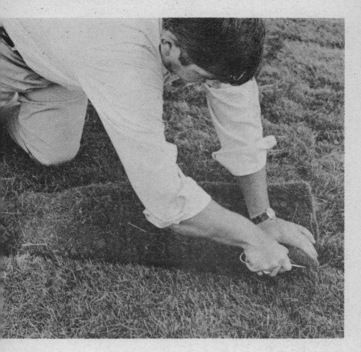

Figure your space carefully before ordering a truck load of sod.

grade job, water runs into your basement, the buried treasure that they didn't remove will rot or work through the turf, the ruts will settle and you will have an uneven lawn with water pockets. They didn't roll the sod, so it separates and dries out on the ends. So all in all, what deal?

To lay sod, buy from a reputable dealer. Next, prepare the lawn in exactly the same way as you would for seeding a new lawn—including rolling, watering for the first week, mowing at the end of ten days, feeding at the end of the first month and continuing a regular lawn program.

To determine how many rolls of sod you will need for your yard, multiply the length by the width and divide by nine. The answer is how many rolls to buy. Be sure to subtract the area of buildings and walks.

Lawn Problems

Dog Damage

Dog damage or urine burn can be repaired by applying a handful of gypsum to the affected area after scratching up the soil, then reseeding. To prevent this damage, apply gypsum at a rate of fifty pounds over 1,000 square yards where the animals run, in early spring.

Green Moss

Green moss is usually found on the north side of trees and buildings and is the result of lack of sunlight or poor drainage. Punch holes in the area and apply gypsum at fifty pounds per 500 square feet. It may be necessary to tile the area if the water problem is too bad.

Too Much Shade

I have never yet found a grass that I can guarantee will grow in the shade, not even the ones that claim to do fairly well. You might try sowing a variety of the rye grasses under trees and then adding a small amount of new seed every couple of weeks.

Soggy Spots

Repair soggy spots by cutting through them on three sides of the sod, and gently roll the sod back and fill it with top soil. Press this down firmly, then roll back the sod and press it firmly to the new soil.

Sandy Soil

For sandy soil, add gypsum at fifty pounds per 1,000 square feet along with one yard of clay loam per 1,000 square feet.

Clay Soil

For clay soil add gypsum at fifty pounds per 1,000 square feet and one yard of sand per 1,000 square feet.

Crab Grass

For some reason, folks seem to think they should destroy the plant, which is a waste of time and effort. To beat crab grass, kill the seed before it germinates. In most parts of the country this should be done in February or March. Use a pre-emergence killer.

Devil
Grass

I have found that the best way to beat it is to join it
and make a whole lawn out of it. However, it can also
be controlled with most any of the spot grass and weed
killers.

Quack Grass

Dig, dig, dig, is about the only way, if it is growing in your yard. There are weed killers that can be used for quack grass control in special crops. Check with your nurseryman.

QUACK QUACK

Salt
Damage

To prevent salt damage, apply a five-foot band of gypsum around all walks and drives. This will preserve the lawn against melting rock-salt.

Moles

Moles are nearly blind, but they have a supersensitive sense of hearing. You can control them by creating a noise that is offensive. To do this, bury wine bottles in the mole runs with the necks sticking out at angles. The wind passing over these sends the noise through the runs. The moles are after grubs that are in your soil. Spray the lawn with chlordane to kill the insects.

Jerry, Is That All?

Not really, Benny. All my readers should know about YARD & FRUIT, an all new, very special gardening magazine.

But Jerry, does it include your up-to-date lawn care reminders and tips?

It sure does, and let me tell you more. YARD & FRUIT is a bi-monthly magazine for gardeners with large vision but limited time and space. It will show you how to create a master landscaping plan with fruit for beauty, food and greater property value. You can harvest country-fresh fruit, berries and vegetables from your own rural acre, town lot or city patio. Why not enjoy better health and nutrition—save money too— while raising better produce than money can buy?

YARD & FRUIT articles are packed with expert and detailed information, but are written in non-technical language and are richly illustrated for quick understanding. Read features like these: Grow a living fence that gives you privacy and wonderful food; all about those new, fast-bearing dwarf fruit trees; in-depth culture of everything from apples to zucchini; storing, freezing, and canning produce; the art of pruning simplified; mulches, fertilizers, and more—much more.

Since it's my favorite gardening magazine—and a good way to keep up with me—I recommend you subscribe. The low rate is $3.50 for 1 year, $6.00 for 2 years.

Take advantage of the special offer the editor has made to the readers of my books. Send $4.85 for two whole years, a savings of $4.15 off the single copy price. Your money back, of course, if you're not delighted.

Write to: YARD & FRUIT, Box 1651, Nashville, Tennessee 37202.

Well Jerry, you could say, if a person follows YARD & FRUIT, the grass (and everything else) will be greener on his side of the fence?

Right, Benny my boy! Grow to the head of the class!

How to do <u>almost</u> everything

What are the latest time and money-saving shortcuts for painting, papering, and varnishing floors, walls, ceilings, furniture? (See pages 102-111 of HOW TO DO *Almost* EVERYTHING.) What are the mini-recipes and the new ways to make food—from appetizers through desserts—exciting and delicious? (See pages 165-283.) How-to-do-it ideas like these have made Bert Bacharach, father of the celebrated composer (Burt), one of the most popular columnists in America.

This remarkable new book, HOW TO DO *Almost* EVERYTHING, is a fact-filled collection of Bert Bacharach's practical aids, containing thousands of tips and hints—for keeping house, gardening, cooking, driving, working, traveling, caring for children. It will answer hundreds of your questions, briefly and lucidly.

How to do <u>almost</u> everything

is chock-full of useful information—information on almost everything you can think of, arranged by subject in short, easy-to-read tidbits, with an alphabetical index to help you find your way around —and written with the famed Bacharach touch.

SEND FOR YOUR FREE EXAMINATION COPY TODAY

We invite you to mail the coupon below. A copy of HOW TO DO *Almost* EVERYTHING will be sent to you at once. If at the end of ten days you do not feel that this book is one you will treasure, you may return it and owe nothing. Otherwise, we will bill you $7.95, plus postage and handling. At all bookstores, or write to Simon and Schuster, Dept. S-52, 630 Fifth Ave., New York, N.Y. 10020.

P 66/2